Paper by Kids

Arnold E. Grummer

DILLON PRESS, INC.
Minneapolis, Minnesota 55415

Dedicated to the thousands of kids whose eyes grew wide with wonder as they watched paper being made around the United States and Canada and to Bill Schroeder, John Stagg, and Walter Lypka who were instrumental in getting the show on the road.

Acknowledgments

The staff of the Institute of Paper Chemistry during the sixteen years I was there is the prime contributor to this book. Especially helpful then, and during the recent manuscript preparation, have been the following: Olga Smith, Dr. Russell Parham, Hilka Kaustinen, Jack Hankey, Fred Sweeney, Robert Rae, Lyle Dambruch, Marvin Filz, Paul Van Rossun, Harold Heller, and Robert Fumal.

Thanks are also extended to John Peckham, William C. Krueger, and Robert Miller. And there is my charming wife, Mabe, who has "put butter on the table" while I put words on paper.

Photos, micrographs, and electron micrographs in the second chapter are from the Institute of Paper Chemistry and are the work of Olga Smith, Dr. Russell Parham, Hilka Kaustinen, and John Hankey. Prints were produced by Fred Sweeney and the staff of the institute's photographic laboratories. Other photos, with occasional exceptions, were taken and produced by Kaukauna High School (Kaukauna, WI) art instructors, W.B. Reifsnyder and Richard Huiting. Historical photographs were provided by the Dard Hunter Paper Museum at the Institute of Paper Chemistry.

Revised 1990

© 1980 by Dillon Press, Inc. All rights reserved

Dillon Press, Inc., 242 Portland Avenue South
Minneapolis, Minnesota 55415

Printed in the United States of America
6   7   8   9   10   92   91   90

Library of Congress Cataloging in Publication Data

Grummer, Arnold E. 1923-
  Paper by kids.

  (Doing and learning books)
  SUMMARY: Step-by-step instructions for various methods of making decorative paper using materials found around the house and simple equipment that can be bought or constructed.
  1. Paper making and trade—Juvenile literature.
  [1. Paper making and trade. 2. Handicraft] I. Title.
  II. Series.
  TS1105.5.G78   676'.22   79-22904

ISBN 0-87518-191-0

Contents

Chapter 1

You can make paper right now

Can you make paper like the page you are now reading from?

Can you make paper that you can send to someone as a Christmas or birthday card?

Can you take the label off a can of vegetables or a bottle of catsup and turn it into new paper?

The answer is yes.

You'll be surprised how much fun it is to make paper and the simple equipment needed for it. Maybe the most fun of all will be enjoying the delight of your family and friends in the paper you have made. It's something that not many people know how to make by hand, but with this book you will be able to do it.

You can make paper right now with things that you have around the house. This is all you need:

● A 2-pound coffee can and a 1-pound coffee can. With a can opener, cut the bottom out of the 1-pound can. If you don't have two coffee cans, get two others that are about the same size as coffee cans. One can should have an opening about an inch or so wider than the other.

● Two pieces of window screen, about 7 inches square each.

● Glass jar with lid. An 8-ounce jar for instant coffee is the right size. You can also use a 1-quart canning jar or other glass or plastic container about the same size.

● Sponge. Some sponges soak up water better than others. Choose one that soaks up water really fast.

Fig. 1-1 *Papermaking setup.*

● Six squares of toilet tissue. If each square has two layers, you need only three squares.

● Piece of board. Any piece of board will work as long as it is smooth on one side and at least 4 inches wide by 6 inches long. You can use your kitchen cutting board or a book wrapped in a piece of plastic to protect it.

● Four paper towels. Fold each sheet in half once, and then in half again.

● Piece of thick, thirsty cloth like an old hand towel or a piece of old wool blanket. A dish towel folded like the paper towels or three rags about the size of the pieces of screen will also work.

1. In the sink or a plastic tub, set up the two cans and a piece of screen as shown in figure 1-1. Put the big can on the bottom. Put a piece of screen over the top of the big can. Set the smaller can on top of the screen. Place the smaller can (the one with its bottom cut out) over the middle of the big can's opening so that all water poured into the smaller can will run through the screen into the big can. For added strength, a piece of hardware cloth can be put under the screen.

2. Fill the glass jar about one-third full of water.

3. Pull the toilet tissue apart into small pieces. Drop the pieces into the water in the jar and screw the lid on tight.

4. Shake the jar as hard and fast as you can until you no longer see the pieces of toilet tissue. The pieces will have come apart into tiny fibers in the water.

5. Take off the lid and fill the jar with water to a little more than three-quarters full.

6. With one hand, hold the smaller can in place on the screen. With the other hand, pour the water from the jar into the smaller can, figure 1-2. Pour the water fast. Almost dump it into the top can. Hold the top can tightly against the screen so that the water will not splash out between the screen and the bottom of the top can. But don't hold it down so tight that you bend the screen down into the bottom can. The water will pass through the screen while the little fibers, which once were toilet tissue, will be caught in a layer on the screen.

7. When all the water has drained into the bottom can, carefully lift the top can off the screen. You should

Fig. 1-2 *Hold the top can down firmly on the screen as water and fibers from the tissue are poured rapidly into it.*

see a round layer of wet fibers on the screen, figure 1-3.

8. Carefully lift the screen with the layer of wet fibers off the bottom can.Set it on a thick cloth on a table or counter top. Put the other piece of screen on top of the round layer of fibers.

9. Dampen the sponge and press it down firmly on the top screen

Fig. 1-3 *Tissue fibers are caught on the screen as the water rushes through.*

1-4 *Removing water. The screen and fibers are placed on a piece of thirsty cloth. Another piece of screen is on top of them. The sponge draws water out of the mat of fibers.*

over the fibers, figure 1-4. This will flatten the layer, and the sponge will suck a lot of water out. Wring out the sponge and press down on the fibers again. Do this until you have taken as much water out of the layer of fibers as you can.

10. Carefully lift the screen off the top of the fibers. Lay the four folded paper towels over the layer of fibers. Press a piece of board or a book wrapped in plastic against the paper towels. The towels will pull still more water from the layer of fibers.

11. Lift the wet paper towels from the layer. Do this carefully and slowly, or some fibers may lift up with the towel sheets.

Fig. 1-5 *Carefully and slowly peel the partly dried new paper sheet from the screen.*

12. Peel the wet fiber layer off the screen, figure 1-5. Do this *very* carefully. You may have trouble getting an edge of the layer to come up from the screen. Keep working with your thumbnail or fingernail until you get a little bit of the edge up from the screen. Then you can peel the whole layer off.

13. Put the damp layer of fibers someplace where it is safe and where it will dry. To make it dry quickly, put the layer of fibers between two pieces of dry cloth and press it with a hot iron until dry.

When the paper has dried completely, it will be strong enough to write or draw on.

Fig. 2-1 *The torn edge of a piece of paper magnified 40 times. The pieces sticking up like coconut on vanilla frosting are actually tiny fibers from plants. An arrow points to a fiber that can easily be seen.*

Chapter 2

What paper is

Paper is not solid like metal or plastic. It is, rather, a thin layer of fibers that a papermaker puts down one at a time into a wet mat. This is what you did when you made paper.

In figure 2-1 you can see the separate fibers sticking up out of the torn edge of a piece of paper. Towards the bottom of the photo, beneath the torn edge, is the paper's surface. It is made up of single fibers like the one the arrow points to.

A closer look at the fibers, figure 2-2, shows that they are all tangled up and lie on top of, around, and beneath one another. When you write on paper, your pencil rides across the backs of the fibers. Each fiber carries a part of the mark. When you erase the mark, you are actually rubbing some of the top fibers off.

Fig. 2-2 *The surface of a sheet of paper magnified 360 times. Here you can see how the fibers lie on top of one another in a flat layer.*

Paper looks and feels smooth because it is made up of many tiny fibers. The closest we come to showing a fiber at its actual size is figure 2-3. Between two pins at the left end of the metal clip is a single

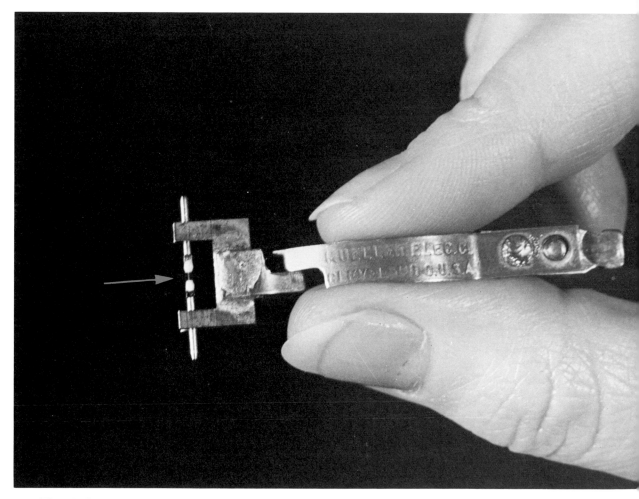

Fig. 2-3 *An arrow points to the tiny papermaking fiber in this photo. Can you see the fiber?*

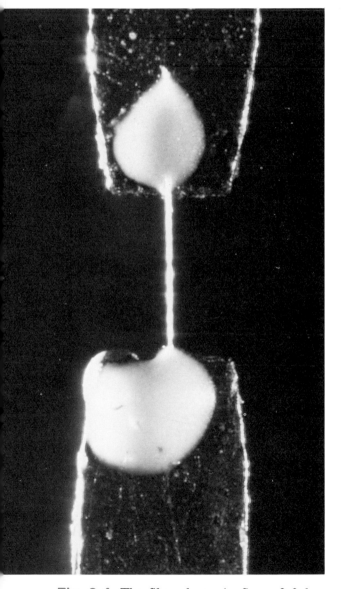

Fig. 2-4 *The fiber shown in figure 2-3 has been magnified 65 times. Note how small it is in comparison to the pins that are holding it.*

papermaking fiber. A laboratory worker at the Institute of Paper Chemistry mounted it there with the aid of a microscope. Scientists then were able to test the fiber's strength. Figure 2-4 is a closeup of the fiber. You can even see the blobs of glue used to hold it to the pins.

The papermaking fiber is cellulose, and it comes from plants. Cellulose fibers make the roots, leaves, and stems of plants strong and rigid. Cellulose is a part of every plant that grows—the flowers in your garden, seaweed in the ocean, and the mighty redwoods of California. Other fibers, such as those in wool, silk, and fiberglass, cannot be used to make paper in the way that most paper is made.

Scientists have spent years studying the cellulose fiber. The more they are able to learn about how it is built and how it works in a living plant, the more they can do with it in making paper.

When scientists first put a cellulose fiber under a powerful microscope, they saw that it was round and that its surface was somewhat rough. Then they found out something interesting.

On the fiber's surface were some round openings called pits. In figure 2-5 you can see these pits in the middle of the fiber. One has been circled. To study them, scientists went to a bigger microscope and magnified one of these tiny openings 10,000 times, figure 2-6. What did they find out? The pits enable the fiber to "eat." Food provided by the plant gets to the inside cells of the fiber by going through the openings in the pits. The cellulose fiber, so small that you can hardly see it, has its own feeding system.

Knowing how small the fiber is, would you believe that it could be hollow down the center? When scientists slice it like a sausage, the slices have no center, figure 2-7. Much like a drinking straw, the fiber

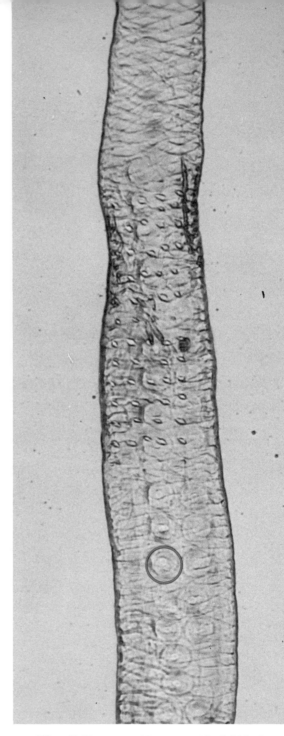

Fig. 2-5 *A wet fiber magnified 300 times.*

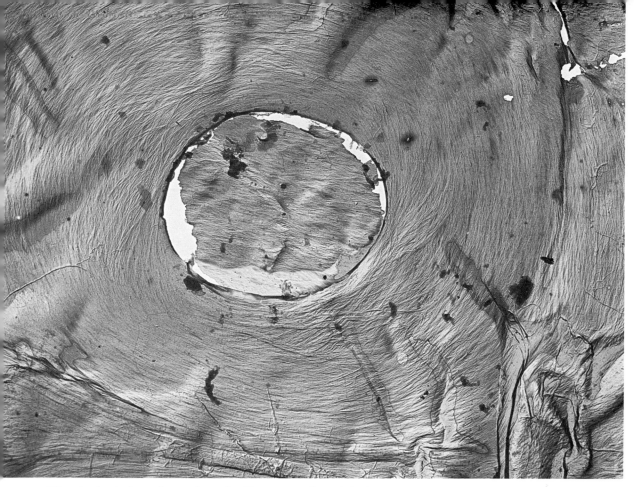

Fig. 2-6 *A pit on the surface of a fiber, magnified 10,000 times. A pit is how a fiber gets food to its inside cells.*

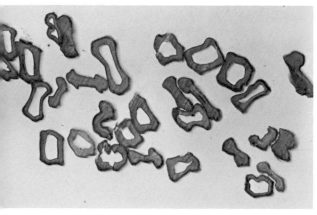

Fig. 2-7 *Slices from a fiber show the fiber is hollow like a drinking straw. These "slices" are magnified 300 times.*

is just a wall around a hollow center.

The fiber's hollowness has meaning. When wet, as it is in a living plant, the fiber is round and its center is open, as shown in figures 2-5 and 2-7. But when dried, the fiber's wall collapses, one side onto the other, closing up the center. It looks thin and narrow like a ribbon, figure 2-8. That is how fibers usually are in paper.

The cellulose fiber is, as you can see, a beautiful part of nature. It has its own feeding system. It changes appearances. It is a little world complete in itself.

When you made paper, you put millions of these fibers together in a thin layer. If you could make yourself small enough, you could find an opening between fibers on the surface of that paper sheet. Then you could crawl into the opening, around and between the fibers inside the sheet, and come out on the other side, figure 2-9. What a trip!

Why don't the fibers fly all over when someone sneezes? You didn't put in glue or anything else to make them stick together when you made paper. Neither do other papermakers. Yet the fibers in paper hang together so tightly that you can write with it, wrap things up in it, and fold it into shapes that stand up by themselves.

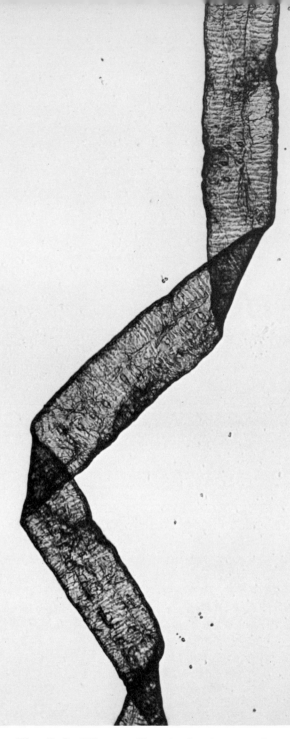

Fig. 2-8 *When a fiber is dried, its hollow center collapses and the fiber, instead of being round, becomes something like a ribbon. The fiber shown here is magnified 200 times.*

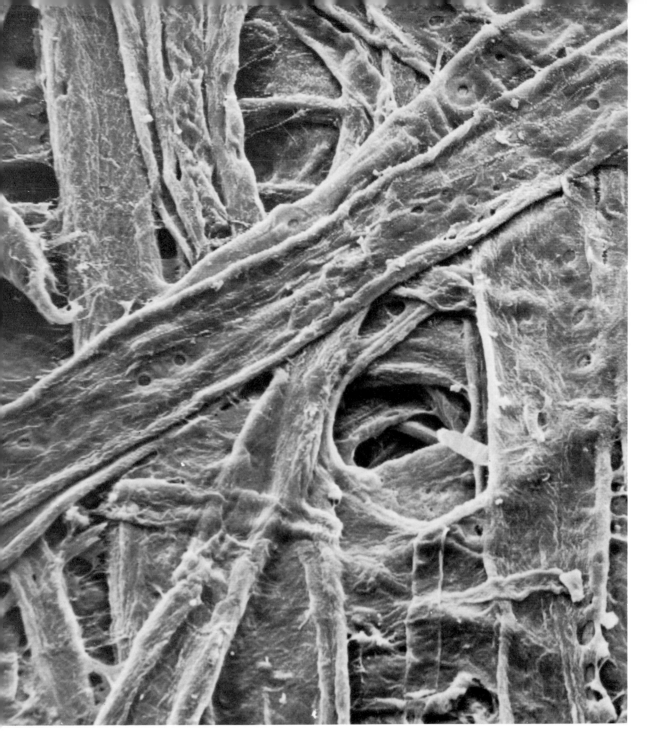

Fig. 2-9 *This is a sheet's surface magnified 920 times. It shows again that paper is a layer of individual fibers. Pick out a fiber and try to imagine it 920 times smaller than shown.*

A miracle happens every time you make paper. The fibers have a built-in hold on one another. Water activates it. Once started, this bond gets stronger as water is taken away. That is some miracle! It takes water to start the bond, but then you have to remove the water to make the bond stronger. If you try to lift the mat of fibers when they are first caught on the screen and are very wet, you will pull some fibers away from the others. After you have removed some of the water, you can lift the mat from the screen. When the mat is dry, it can be handled roughly, and the fibers hang onto one another so strongly that they can be used as paper.

Humans didn't invent the papermaking bond. We just happened to find out about it. This natural bond is the miracle that has made all paper ever made in the world possible.

Will it happen every time you make paper? You can bet your faded blue jeans it will!

In fact, why don't you try it right now? Every piece of paper around you is a source of fibers. Just get the fibers to let go of one another as you did with the toilet tissue.

Loosening fibers in paper and using them to make new paper is called "recycling." That is what happens to the newspapers you pick up when your Boy Scout or Girl Scout troop has a paper drive. Some big paper mills use only fibers from "waste" paper to make their new paper. About one-fifth of all fibers used for papermaking in the United States comes from used paper. You can make new paper from old envelopes, napkins, notes, newspapers, magazines, and cereal boxes.

"But," you may ask, "if I can make new paper from all these things, why in the world did you have me make it from something like toilet tissue? After all, what will my friends say when I tell them, 'Here is a piece of paper I made out of toilet tissue'?"

Some of your friends may not be very impressed, but there was a good reason for asking that toilet tissue be used for your first sheet. The bond between fibers can be loosened more easily in some kinds of paper than in others. If you had used grocery sack paper, for example, you might still be shaking the jar with water and paper in it.

For making new paper from tough paper like grocery sacks, you need a real ripping, pulling, tearing chewer of some type. Something like that is likely to be in your house. Did you ever see what your kitchen blender does to eggs, tomatoes, nuts, and even ice? It will do the same thing to paper.

When paper is put into water in a blender and the blender is turned on, the blade goes around very fast and tears the fibers apart from one another. The water helps the blade. If it is true that fibers hang on more strongly as water is taken away, it is equally true that they hang on more weakly as water is added. That is why most wet paper has no strength. If you want cellulose fibers to let go of one another, make them wet.

To make a sheet of paper that is not from toilet tissue, set up the equipment you used in chapter 1 and do the following steps.

1.   Select some paper for fibers. Newspaper is a good choice for the first sheet because its fibers come apart quite easily. In chapter 6, all types of paper will be discussed for recycling.

2.   For the right amount of paper to recycle, take the top can, place it on the paper, and draw a circle around its bottom. Cut out the circle. That amount of paper will make a new sheet of about the same thickness. For a thicker sheet, use more paper. For a thinner sheet, use less.

3.   Because some fibers will get lost in recycling, cut out a quarter of another circle. Add it to the other piece of paper.

4.   Put just enough water in the blender to cover the blade, figure 2-10. With too much water, the paper will stay away from the blade.

5.   Cut the paper into small pieces and drop them into the blender. Be sure to put the lid on before turning the blender on! If you don't, wet fibers and bits of wet paper will be thrown all over the room and you.

6.   Let the blender run for about a minute or until you can't see pieces of paper anymore.

7.   Add water until the blender is about three-fourths full.

8.   Put the top can on the screen. Pour the fibers and water into the

Fig. 2-10 *Notice how little water is put in the blender. It's just enough to cover the blade.*

top can and make paper as you did before.

Did people always learn how to make paper with used coffee cans and toilet tissue? No. Food cans were not invented until about 1812. Toilet tissue like today's was not invented until about 1907. Paper, on the other hand, has been made since 105. In the next chapter, we'll take a short look at paper history. After learning how people made paper in the past and what they used, you may want to use only toilet tissue and cans again when teaching someone else how to make paper.

Chapter 3

How a papermaker makes paper

To make paper, it is necessary to have three things: sieve, fibers, and water. When these three things are combined in the right way, the result is paper.

The first person to make paper was most probably Ts'ai Lun, a man in the court of the Chinese emperor. Ts'ai Lun combined the three things about the same way you did when making your sheet. Since he poured water with fibers in it through a sieve, the process he used became known as the "pour" method.

Papermakers gave it a name because they later developed a way to make paper in which the fibers and water were not poured. Instead, the fibers and water were put into a vat. Then the sieve was dipped into the vat to get the water and fibers on it. When the sieve was lifted out, the water and fibers were kept on its surface by a frame around the sieve's edge. This made the water run down through the sieve. The fibers were caught on the surface, forming a sheet. This was called the "dip" method of papermaking.

The dip method was soon used by most papermakers. It was the method used by all hand papermakers in Europe and the United States. But some papermakers in Siam, Tibet, and other places kept on using the pour method.

This book deals mainly with the pour method. The equipment is easier to make, a better piece of paper can be made with less practice and experience, and a lot of pulp does not have to be prepared to make just one sheet.

When you make a sheet, you will

continue a very old craft. It is about as old as our calendar for telling the date. The date on our calendar now reads 1980. Ts'ai Lun made the first paper in 105. That is a long history!

Hand Mold

The papermaker's chief tool has always been the sieve, which is called a hand mold. In the past, the mold has been made of several different things and in several different ways. All that was necessary was that it be able to strain fibers out of water.

The first mold was probably made by stretching a piece of cloth between the sides of a bamboo frame. But soon, changes were made.

In the Orient, the sieves became woven mats of reeds, grasses, or finely cut bamboo. The mats rested on wooden ribs in a frame. After the mold was dipped into a vat, the mat could be lifted from the frame for the next steps in papermaking.

When wire was invented in Europe, it was used instead of the reeds, grasses, and bamboo strips. It was strung in strands from one side of a frame to the other. A second frame was built to fit around the first. It was later called the "deckle." This hand mold was also dipped into a vat.

Around 1750, papermakers began to use woven wire for their molds. Instead of strands running in one direction, it was like the screen you used to make your sheet. Papermakers changed to woven wire because they believed it gave paper a smoother surface for printing. Paper made on molds with wires running in just one direction is called "laid." Paper made on molds with woven wire is called "wove."

Papermakers in the United States used both laid and wove molds. First they were all imported from

This is Marchand Warrell, who lived almost two hundred years ago in England. He helped run one of the first paper machines. Warrell is wearing a hat of folded paper, which old-time papermakers made themselves to keep their hair out of their work.

Europe. Just before the Revolutionary War, Isaac Langle and Nathan Sellers started making them in the United States.

Molds began to lose out when a Frenchman, Nicholas-Louis Robert invented a paper machine in 1798. It made paper faster than workers could do it by hand. Soon hand papermakers had less and less to do. Mold makers also had less and less work. Papermakers and mold makers in Europe dwindled to just a handful. In the United States, they disappeared altogether.

But for more than fifteen hundred years, every bit of paper used in the world was made by hand. Someone bent his or her back to dip every sheet.

ning off the sides rather than through it. The raised edge is called the deckle, and it is a part of every hand mold.

Your deckle was the small can put on top of the screen. It kept the water from running all over. It also determined the size and shape of the sheet. If your deckle had been a square can, your sheet would have been square.

In the pour method, the deckle can be quite high. In the dip method, the deckle may not rise more than a quarter of an inch around the edges of the sieve.

So when people speak of a hand mold, they are talking about some type of a sieve material with a deckle around it.

Deckle

There has always been a raised edge around the sieve of a mold to keep the water and fibers from run-

Fibers

Fibers from all kinds of plants have been used for papermaking. Sometimes in the past, papermakers got their fibers directly from plants. At other times, fibers were taken from old cloth, rope, or other things that plants had been made into.

For many years in Europe and the United States, only rags were used by papermakers. They didn't know how to make paper from anything else. The rags were worn-out clothes made from linen, which came from flax plants, or cotton, which was also a plant product.

If you read a newspaper in colonial days, you might have seen want ads placed by papermakers offering to buy rags. You might have received three pennies a pound for them. In those days, three pennies bought much more than they do today. Benjamin Franklin was one of the rag buyers and sellers. He helped start a number of paper mills.

Because there were not enough rags in the colonies, they were imported from England, Germany, Italy, Egypt, and other countries.

One papermaker said he could tell which country the rags came from by how clean or dirty they were.

Rags played an important part in paper manufacture for more than five hundred years in Europe and North America. A little poem was made up about them.

Rags make paper,
Paper makes money,
Money makes banks,
Banks make loans,
Loans make beggars,
Beggars make rags.

People still prize "rag content" paper today.

Getting Fibers

It has never been easy to get fibers from plants themselves or from things, like rags, that plants have been made into.

In plants, fibers are held together by a cement-like substance that the plant produces as it grows. To get the fibers, papermakers have to rip them from each other by force, or cook the plants in chemicals until the cement softens and lets the fibers come apart from each other.

Fibers have been ripped apart usually by stamping or grinding plants while wet. Papermakers first did this with a "mortar and pestle" arrangement. Later, machinery was developed. Today, your newspaper is made with fibers ripped apart by forcing a length of log against a grindstone. The fibers are called "groundwood pulp."

Chemicals were used to attack the plant's structure even in the early days of stamping and grinding. Before being stamped or ground, the plants were soaked in lime pits or in water in which ashes had been soaked. Today, fibers can be gotten from trees by the use of chemicals alone.

But in Europe, rags, ropes, and cloth sacks were mostly stamped. Huge stampers run by waterwheels were used at first. Then a more efficient machine, known as a beater was invented in Holland. It was called a "Hollander."

Rags To Wood

When did European and American papermakers switch from rags to wood and other plants for making paper? Around 1850. Why? Because there weren't enough rags anymore to make all the paper people wanted. That made scientists get busy and try to find something else from which to make paper.

All this time, papermakers in the Orient were already making paper from plants. But papermakers in the Western World didn't know about it.

The scientists in Europe and the United States worked very hard.

They tried many plants. They even made experimental paper from things like algae and cow dung. Soon paper was being made from straw. But eventually a way was found to make paper from trees, first by grinding them, and then by cooking them in chemicals. Trees are more or less big bundles of fibers. Papermakers have not had trouble with a shortage of fibers since.

Besides rags and plants, fibers have always been available from used paper. All paper is fiber. When paper is through being used for a letter or anything else, the fibers are still good. Fibers in paper can be taken apart much more easily than those in trees and used again.

How Papermaking Spread

The first paper was made in China, probably in A.D. 105. The fibers came from the bark of the mulberry tree, hemp, fishnets, and rags, according to official Chinese chronicles.

Papermaking did not leave lands ruled by China until more than six hundred years later. In A.D. 751, a battle was fought at Samarkand between the Chinese and Arabians. Some Chinese papermakers were taken prisoner by the Arabians. From them, the Arabians learned how to make paper. The secret of papermaking was kept in the Arabian countries until 1151, when a paper mill was built in Xativa, Spain. It was the first paper mill in Europe.

It took another four hundred years for papermaking to cross the Atlantic Ocean. Do you think the United States was the first place to have papermaking in North America? It wasn't. It was Mexico. People from Spain brought it there to a city called Culhuacan, in 1575.

Did it *ever* get to the United

States? It finally did. In the year 1690, the first paper mill in what is now the United States was set up in Germantown, Pennsylvania.

The first picture ever made of paper-making, which appeared in 1528. The papermaker is using a dip hand mold in a round wooden vat. Behind him is a press for squeezing water out of wet sheets. At left are the stampers that stamped rags into little fibers. Through the window can be seen waterwheels that provided power for the stampers. In front, an apprentice is carrying away a stack of newly made sheets.

Today

Today, the old craft of making paper by hand is being learned anew. At least one full-time handmade paper mill is operating in the United States. It is the Twinrocker mill in Brookston, Indiana. Students, printers, artists, and craftsmen in many places are making or buying molds and making their own paper. Hand papermakers have held conferences in different parts of the country.

Old items from papermaking's past can be seen in a museum. It is the Dard Hunter Paper Museum at the Institute of Paper Chemistry in Appleton, Wisconsin.

When you start making paper by hand, you reach back through centuries into old, old times. You pick up a craft that has been going on for more than 1,850 years.

Chapter 4

Make a mold

Now that you know you can make paper, it is time to move up to a good hand mold. This chapter tells you how to build one and then describes some fancy touches. The extra details will take a bit more work and materials but will probably make a better hand mold. Read the whole chapter before starting so that those details you want can be included in your hand mold.

The mold suggested is a pour mold. It is easy for kids to use and it makes good paper with very little practice. You can decide how thick your paper will be by putting the right amount of pulp into the deckle. Many kinds of experiments in papermaking can be done with it. It can make paper as fine as any other hand mold can. (If you would rather buy a mold, see the appendix, page 107, for ordering information.)

Building the Mold

As projects go, building the mold is not difficult. Mostly, you have to handle a saw, screwdriver, and hammer, and be able to pound a nail straight. If needed, help might come from one of your parents or

weather stripping

Fig. 4-1 *A hand mold you can build yourself.*

from an industrial arts teacher at school.

Look at the mold in figure 4-1 and note the following things. It is made of two square wooden frames that are joined by a hinge. The bottom edges of the left-hand frame are covered with weather stripping. This will make a watertight joint when the two frames are swung together. The frames can be locked together with the hook on the left-hand frame and the eye on the

right-hand frame. A piece of screen covers the opening of the right-hand frame, making this frame the sieve. The left-hand frame is the deckle part of the mold.

Materials

- 1 x 6 board, 5 feet long
- ¼-inch or ½-inch self-adhesive weather stripping, 2 feet long
- 1 piece hardware cloth, 7 inches square

- 1 piece aluminum or nylon window screen, 7 inches square
- 1 1½-inch hinge
- 1 1½-inch hook and eye
- Nails, tacks, or staples

To begin, cut the following from a 1 x 6 board or other lumber that is ¾-inch thick:

Pieces	Length	Width
2	7½ in.	3 in.
2	7½ in.	2 in.
2	6 in.	3 in.
2	6 in.	2 in.

Building the Deckle

1.   Using the 3-inch wide pieces of wood, build a square frame. As shown in figure 4-2, put the shorter pieces between the ends of the long pieces. Nail them together. If you are a good carpenter, they can be glued or doweled together.

2.   Put self-adhesive weather stripping on the edges of one side of the frame, figure 4-3. It is easy to put on. Put the sticky side down on the edges of the frame. Be sure the frame's edges are clean before you put the stripping on.

Fig. 4-2 *The frame for the deckle, ready to be nailed.*

Fig. 4-3 *The black strip on the top edge of this frame is weather stripping. It makes a watertight joint between the two frames of the hand mold.*

3. If you can, put a board and weight on top of the weather stripping while you build the sieve. It will help the stripping to stick well.

Building the Sieve

1. Using the 2-inch wide pieces of wood, build square frame 2 in the same way that square frame 1 was built. Again, put the short pieces of wood between the ends of the long pieces. When finished, square frame 2 should match square frame 1 perfectly, except for the width of wood. Both squares should have a 6-inch square opening.

2. Cut a piece of hardware cloth 7 inches square. Tack or staple it over the opening on one side of

Fig. 4-4 *Hardware cloth stapled to the frame of the sieve.*

square frame 2, figure 4-4. Use small staples or short tacks with wide heads. A staple gun can be used.

3. Cut a piece of aluminum or nylon window screen 7 inches square. Put the screen down on top of the hardware cloth. Keeping the screen stretched smooth, tack or staple it down over the hardware cloth.

Hinge, Hook, and Eye

1. Place frame 2 on your workbench with the screen side up. On top of it, place frame 1 with the weather stripping side down. This should bring the weather stripping

and screen together. Line the frames up with each other perfectly. Attach the hinge at the middle of one of the four sides as shown in figure 4-5.

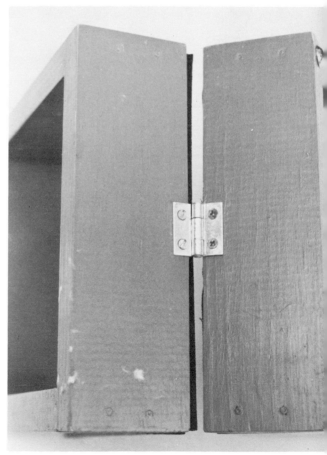

Fig. 4-5 *Placement of the hinge to hold the two frames together.*

Fig. 4-6 *Placement of the hook and eye.*

2. On the side opposite the hinge, also in the middle, put a hook and eye, figure 4-6. Put the hook on the deckle and the eye on the sieve frame. Take care in how far apart they are placed. When hooked, they should hold the deckle and sieve shut firmly, but the fit should not be so tight that you have trouble pushing the hook into the eye.

Paint

Paint your mold. Paint will prevent water from damaging it. You can paint at this point when the mold is finished, or you can paint the frames as soon as they are finished and before weather stripping and hardware cloth are put on.

Extra Touches

Papermaking Wire

Screen that has smaller openings than window screen can be purchased. The size of opening in a screen depends on the screen's "mesh." The mesh size is a number that tells how many wires there are per inch. The more wires there are crowded into an inch of screen, the smaller the openings between them. In the past hand papermakers used about a 20-mesh screen. It had 20 wires in an inch of screen.

Window screen usually has a mesh of about 8. Since there is quite a bit of space between the wires, some papermaking fibers will get through. Certain kinds of fibers may get stuck in the openings and stay there when a newly formed sheet is lifted from the screen.

You may want to use screen with smaller mesh like that used in the paper industry. If so, you can order it from a company that makes screen for the industry. An address is given in the appendix, page 107.

You may also be able to get some screen from a paper mill if you live near one. If you do not know someone working there, call and ask to speak to someone in public relations. Explain what you are doing and state that it would be helpful if you could get some paper-making wire for your hand mold. Be brief and polite because you are taking up some person's time. The paper mill is a busy place, but the people there will generally provide help if they can.

A Loose Screen

Instead of stapling or tacking your screen down over the hardware cloth, it can be laid there loose. Handle it in the same way you handled the screen when making paper with the coffee cans. Different kinds of screens can be used at different times. The hand mold will close just as easily when the screen is laid loose over the hardware cloth as when it is tacked down or stapled.

Cloth as a Screen

Rather than using metal screen for a sieve, use a piece of cloth. It can be laid over the hardware cloth just as a screen can be. It will be held firmly in place when the hand mold is closed. Keep it stretched tightly as you close the mold. Look for cloth that lets water run through easily. Experimenting with different kinds of cloth is fun.

Fig. 4-7 *How to put ribs in your hand mold.*

Ribs

More support for the screen can be built into your hand mold. One way is to put another layer of hardware cloth over the first one. A second way is to put in "ribs." Dip hand molds used by European and colonial hand papermakers had ribs.

Figure 4-7 shows one way to put in ribs. Bolts through the frame's sides hold a metal plate on the two walls of the frame. The metal plate is a ledge upon which thin metal ribs rest. Slots hold the ribs upright.

Putting ribs into a mold is difficult. They are mentioned here mostly to let you know what they are, rather than to encourage you to put them in your hand mold. Ribs give extra support for the screen, but you do not need them to make good paper with your hand mold.

Chapter 5

Using the hand mold

Now you are ready to put your hand mold to work and make a sheet of paper. When finished, your sheet should be about 6 inches by 6 inches and ready to carry a neat note, a birthday greeting, or your family's grocery list.

Water and a Vat

Tap water, hard or soft, works. Make sure that the water is clean to prevent dirt from getting into your paper. Hand papermakers of the past used the purest water they could find from clear, sparkling streams. You can get pure water from a dehumidifier or by letting the dirt settle out of rain water.

Your vat should be at least 14 inches wide. The sides must be as high as the top of the hand mold when it is set in the vat. A plastic vat is best because it does not rust. Rust ruins paper. My vat is a round plastic dishpan that is 14 inches in diameter with sides 8 inches high, and I bought it in a discount store. Hand papermakers have used vats of all shapes and sizes made of wood or metal. To prevent rust, metal vats were often lined with lead. You can use a metal pan, pail, or tub if you can keep it from rusting, or even the kitchen sink.

Couch Materials

In papermaking, "couch" is pronounced "kootch." It means taking the wet fiber mat off the screen and removing water at the same time.

Couch materials absorb water. Hand papermakers use specially woven wool blankets called felts. You can buy felts from an address given in the appendix, page 106. You can also try pieces of an old wool blanket or other thick cloth that absorbs water and is smooth.

Felts do not always work well with pour hand molds. Blotter paper works better. Office supply stores sell several sizes of desk blotters. From the 24 x 36-inch size, you can cut twelve 8-inch square pieces. You can also buy blotter sheets made especially for couching. (See the appendix, page 107.) When kept clean and dried after use, couch sheets can be reused.

The Papermaking Process

Materials
- Piece of cloth, 8 inches square. Get "open" cloth like cheesecloth or gauze.
- Sponge: one that really soaks up water.
- Couch sheets: at least 12 pieces of blotter paper, 8 inches square. Build up your supply to 30 or 40 couch sheets. Or try wool blanket or thick cloth pieces.
- Rolling pin
- Fibers: recycle any one of the following as explained in chapter 2—
  3 pieces newspaper, 6 inches square
  2 ¾ pieces facial tissue
  1 piece of any paper about the thickness of a page in this book, 6 x 9 inches

Forming the Sheet

1. Lock the two frames of the mold together with the hook and eye.

2. Fill the vat with about 5 inches of water. Set the mold, sieve frame down, in the vat. The water should not be higher than the hand mold. The water inside the deckle should

rise almost to its top, figure 5-1.

3.   Hold the mold on the vat's bottom with one hand. With the other,

Fig. 5-2 *Pouring the fibers into the deckle.*

pour the recycled fibers into the water inside the deckle, figure 5-2.

4.   Spread the fibers around evenly in the deckle by putting your

Fig. 5-1 *Water should rise almost to the top of the deckle when the mold is placed into the vat.*

Fig. 5-3 *Spreading the fibers evenly in the deckle.*

fingers in the water and wiggling them very fast, figure 5-3. That action riffles the water, which spreads the fibers. Wiggle your fingers until you see that the fibers are spread evenly.

5. Lift the mold straight up out of

Fig. 5-4 *The mold is lifted straight up to allow the water to drain and leave fibers in an even layer on the sieve.*

the vat, figure 5-4. Hold it level until water stops draining through the sieve. For some kinds of fibers, water will drain quickly. For others, it will drain very slowly.

6. Drain more water by lowering one corner of the hand mold, figure 5-5. Keep the corner lowered until water stops draining.

Fig. 5-5 *After the fibers have landed on the screen, the mold is held with one corner low so that more water drains out.*

Fig. 5-6 *A mat of single fibers on the sieve forms a wet sheet.*

7. Set the mold on your workbench or table top. Unlatch the two frames. Raise the top frame and you will see the sheet you have formed, figure 5-6

Couching

1. Place the mold where the deckle can lean against something.

That will keep the sieve frame flat on the table top, figure 5-7.

2. Carefully put two blotters over the new sheet, figure 5-8. Press your palms all over the top blotter until water comes through, figure 5-9.

Fig. 5-7 *Leaning the deckle against something lets the screen lie flat on a surface.*

Fig. 5-8   *Couch sheets are placed carefully on top of the mat of wet fibers.*

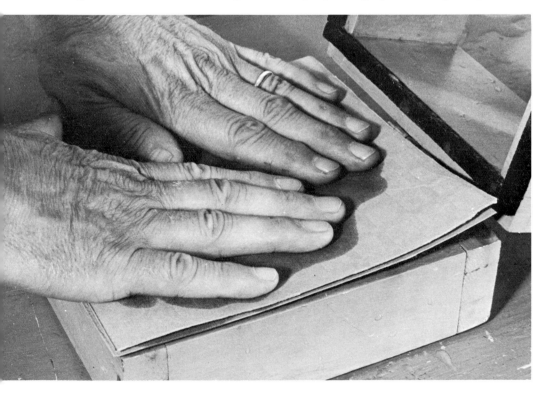

Fig. 5-9 *Apply pressure to couch sheets with your hands.*

3. When water shows through the top blotter, wet your sponge, wring it out, and press it all over the top of the blotter, figure 5-10. Press and wring the sponge until it draws no more water. The new sheet should now be ready to be lifted off the screen with the couch sheets.

4. Slowly lift one corner of the couch sheets, figure 5-11. If the new sheet lifts from the screen, keep on lifting. If it does not, try lifting at other corners and places until you find one where the new sheet lifts.

Note: Some recycled fibers lift easily; others, like those from facial tissue, may stick to the screen. This happens with mesh as large as window screen. If the new sheet does not lift, remove the couch sheet. Then try to raise one of the new sheet's corners with your fingers and slowly lift it off. If some of the new sheet lifts with the couch sheets and some sticks to the screen, try lifting at another place. Even if some fibers stick to the wire, the new sheet may be all right after drying. If nothing works, wash the fiber off the screen. Recycle a different kind of paper and try again.

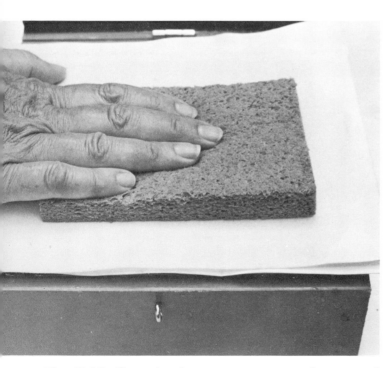

Fig. 5-10 *Squeezing down on a sponge over the wet couch sheets removes more water.*

Fig. 5-11 *Lifting the mat of fibers off the sieve.*

Pressing

1. On a clean, flat surface, lay the couch sheet down with the new sheet facing up. Put a piece of thin, open cloth, like cheesecloth or gauze, carefully over the new sheet. Press a sponge down on the

cloth over the entire surface, figure 5-12. Press and wring the sponge until it draws no more water.

2. Carefully peel the new sheet from the couch sheet, figure 5-13, and place it between two dry couch

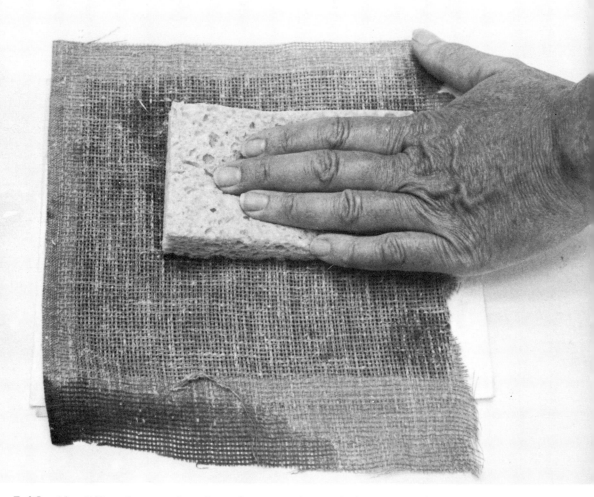

Fig. 5-12 *After lifting the new sheet from the screen, lay a cloth over it and use the sponge again.*

Fig. 5-13 *Peel the new sheet carefully off the couch sheet.*

sheets. If the sheet is too weak to be peeled off, remove more water with the sponge. If it is still not strong enough to be moved, leave it on the wet couch sheet and put both sheets between two dry couch sheets. Peel the new sheet off after completing step 3.

3. To squeeze out more water, roll a rolling pin over the couch sheets, figure 5-14. Practice will show you how hard you can press. Too much pressure will force the wet fibers apart. Too little pressure will fail to squeeze out water. After going over the sheet once with the rolling pin, check to see if it is damaged. If not, roll with more pressure. Fibers from some kinds of paper can take a lot of pressure. Fibers from others can take very little. Roll over the couch sheets four or five times.

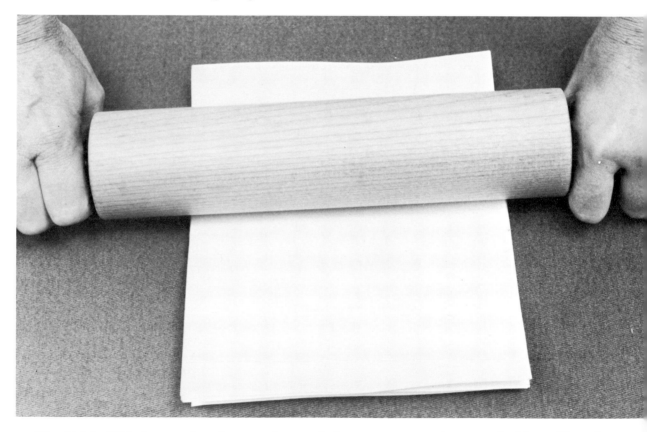

Fig. 5-14 *With the new sheet between dry couch sheets, more water is removed with a rolling pin.*

Drying

Drying can be done by one of several methods. If you want to dry the paper quickly, use method 1. Fast drying may result in a crinkled or puckered sheet. For a smooth sheet, dry by method 2. Or use some of both in method 3.

Method 1: Take the new sheet from between the wet couch sheets. Place it on an ironing board and put a thin, open piece of cloth such as cheesecloth or gauze over it. Iron with a very hot iron until dry. Move the iron very slowly over the sheet, but watch for scorching. Turn the sheet over every 1½ minutes. Drying will take 4 to 5 minutes. If you don't like the marks gauze or cheesecloth makes on the sheet, use cloth with a smoother surface.

Method 2: Separate the wet couch sheets and put the new sheet between two dry couch sheets. Put the dry couch sheets on a flat surface and stack weights on top. Bricks, heavy pans, books, or a clothes iron are some of the things you can use. A piece of plastic under the couch sheets and another on top will keep the flat surface and weights dry. Every four hours exchange the damp couch sheets for dry ones until the new sheet is dry.

Method 3: Iron the sheet until it is almost dry as in method 1. Then complete the drying by putting the sheets under weights as in method 2.

Other Methods: Dry the new sheet on a hot surface. Photographic print dryers work although the sheet may pucker. Or try drying the sheet on a board in the sun (see Chapter 9, Drying on a Board and in a Press).

Making Paper with a Loose Screen

Paper can be formed on any screen or sieve laid on top of your mold's

Fig. 5-15 *Remove the loose screen from the mold by gripping its upper corners.*

screen or directly on top of the hardware cloth. If you did not tack down the screen when you made your mold, it can lie there during papermaking without being fastened. That way you can use different mesh screens or even pieces of cloth that will let water through.

Screens to just "lay on" can be cut 7 ½ inches square. Cloth sieves can be cut 8 inches square.

To make paper, lay the screen or cloth on the screen or hardware cloth of your mold. Latch the mold's frames together. Follow the method given under Forming the Sheet, page 41. Then couch as follows:

1. Lift the screen by taking hold of its two top corners, figure 5-15.

Fig. 5-16 *To couch the sheet off the screen, put the screen's bottom edge on a couch sheet and gently drop the top edge toward you.*

2.   Holding the screen straight up, put its bottom edge on a couch sheet, figure 5-16.

3.   Lower the screen so that the new sheet is put against the couch sheet.

4.   Take out water by putting a sponge down on the screen. Sponge over the entire surface of the new sheet.

5.   Raise the screen slowly, leaving the new sheet on the couch sheet. If fibers stick to the screen, see the note under step 4 of Couching, page 48.

6.   Press and dry the sheet as usual.

Chapter 6

New paper from old

In the past, papermakers have gotten fibers from just about everything that grows. In a book published in 1864, Joel Munsell gave a list of things that have been used to make paper "of fair qualities." Here are some items from the list in his book, *A Chronology of Paper and Papermaking:*

Asparagus	Hornet's nests
Bamboo	Lily of the valley
Bark	Moss
Cabbage stumps	Peat
Corn husks	Seaweed

Today, the paper industry gets most of its fibers from trees and other growing plants through a process called pulping. Pulping is hard to do and takes a long time. Since it requires chemicals, it can be dangerous. In the appendix, page 106, you will find the addresses of companies that will sell pulp in dry lap form to you. You can, however, use fibers that have already been pulped, and you don't have to buy them.

Instead of new fibers, make paper with used fibers. Every piece of paper on earth is made up of used fibers. Separate them and you can use them to make new paper. They are as good as new fibers for most purposes, and better for some. For no money at all, you can get all you want.

Used paper is called wastepaper, but don't let the word "waste" fool you. Some greeting cards, wedding announcements, and paper sacks have the finest fibers available. Why throw them away? By recycling, use them to make new paper from old.

Why Does Recycling Work?

In chapter 2 you read that fibers hang onto each other more strongly as water is taken away. The reverse is true, too. Add water to paper, and the bonds between the fibers get weaker.

See this for yourself. Take two squares of one-ply, or one square of two-ply, bathroom tissue. Stack three quarters in the middle of the squares. Pick up the four corners and lift. The bathroom tissue will lift the quarters.

Now pour one teaspoon of water over the quarters. Again take the four corners and lift. The tissue will tear. What is the difference between the first lift and the second? Water. In the second lift, water has weakened the bond between fibers. As they let go of each other, the paper tears.

Recycling works because water weakens the bond between fibers and lets them separate. Some fibers get used three or four times.

The paper industry uses Hydra-pulpers for recycling. In some ways, a Hydrapulper is a big blender.

How to Pick Paper for Recycling

If you put just any and all kinds of paper in the blender, the recycled fibers will probably make gray paper. Recycling paper with print or pictures on it will make gray paper. Recycling papers of a number of different colors often results in gray paper.

White Paper

For white paper, recycle only paper with no printing or writing on either side. Cut out the unprinted parts from envelopes and cards and the margins of newspapers and magazine pages. Watch for white grocery sacks. If it is worth it to you, buy some bond typewriter paper. Twenty-five percent bond paper has twenty-five percent cotton fibers. Fifty percent bond has fifty percent. It is very good fiber.

Colored Paper

Colored desk blotters can provide fibers in different colors. Other sources are Christmas cards and their envelopes, advertisements, stationery, paper bags, construction paper, and posters. Keep a "bank" of colored fibers by setting up big brown envelopes in which to put different-colored used paper—red, blue, green, orange, purple, and so forth. See chapter 8 for dyeing fibers.

Strong Paper

Paper companies make strong paper from long and/or well-beaten fibers. You can find these fibers in grocery sacks, wrapping paper, and good writing paper. You usually have to run them longer in the blender. Strong paper cannot be made from tissues, newspapers, comic books, or paperback book pages. Some greeting cards make weak new paper. Experimenting will soon show you which papers to use for new strong paper.

Decorative Paper

Run your blender for less time than it takes to make all the paper pieces disappear. Part of the paper will have become fibers and part will still be bits of paper. When you make paper from this mixture, the new sheet will have little pieces of paper on its surface. Recycling papers with different colors printed on it can give you a speckled or flecked sheet. Try food can labels having many colors, such as V-8 Cocktail Vegetable Juice. Try napkins or blotters of different colors, colored comic strips, and colorful candy bar wrappers. Cut up part of a gold foil margarine wrapper and put the pieces into the blender with cut up paper. The new sheet will have gold flecks. Try used postage stamps. To experiment, run your blender different lengths of time. Remember, some used papers come apart faster than others.

Review of Sources

Following is a list of kinds of paper that can be used for recycling.

gift wrapping paper	grocery sacks
ticket stubs	blotters
postage stamps	newspapers
calendars	comic books
matchbook covers	crepe paper
advertisements	envelopes
construction paper	playing cards
magazines	tissues
Cracker Jack boxes	boxes
letters	labels
candy bar wrappers	wasp nests

Wasp nests? Yes, don't forget wasp nests. The wasp is said to be the world's first papermaker. A French naturalist named Réaumur explained how they did it in *Notes on the History of Insects*, a book he wrote in 1719.

Réaumur saw wasps go to the face of weathered boards. They took little bits of wood and chewed them. It seemed that wasps had something in their saliva that freed cellulose fibers from other wood parts. They were also able to waterproof the paper. Réaumur gave high praise to a kind of wasp that lived in Canada. "At first glance," he wrote, "one would accept the nest as the work of man." Réaumur's book eventually gave European and American papermakers the idea that they could make paper from trees. Before this, they had used only linen and cotton rags.

So don't forget wasp nests when it comes to recycling. Just be very, very sure that there are no wasps at home before you help yourself to a nest! If the nest makes weak paper, mix the fibers half and half with fibers from brown grocery sacks. Or use a mixture of one-quarter sack fibers and three-quarters nest fibers.

The only hard-and-fast rule we can offer is not to recycle any paper that someone else has a use for. That's why it's a good idea to look first in your own wastebasket!

How to Recycle Fibers

Use the method given in chapter 2, page 21, but change the amount of paper you recycle for your hand mold. To make a new sheet of average thickness, cut up used paper equal to 1½ times the size of the inside of the deckle. The inside of the deckle is the size your new sheet will be. It is 6 inches square, so cut up paper to measure 6 x 9 inches. If you want new paper that

is thicker, cut up more. It you want thinner paper, cut up less.

Soak the used paper for an hour or more before putting it into the blender. It will come apart more easily and more completely. This is especially true for wrapping papers, paper sacks, and other strong papers.

Recycling Projects

To begin recycling, try these two projects. As in the paper industry, fibers for papermaking are called pulp.

Project 1: Globs and Blobs of Color

In your blender, reduce colored paper napkins or blotters only half-way to fibers. Experiment with different amounts of colors. Try colored tissues. Run the blender for longer and shorter times. The

Fig. 6-1 *The spots you see in this sheet are pieces of colored napkins and blotters.*

sheets made will show the different colored clumps of fiber, figure 6-1. Using only napkins or blotters will work, but adding white pulp recycled from stronger paper will give the sheet more strength. Later, try making a sheet from only napkins, blotters, and tissues.

Materials
● White pulp for ¼ to ⅓ of a sheet (3 strips of 1 x 6-inch white paper will make enough pulp)
● Napkins or blotters of three different colors

1. Make the white pulp as described in chapter 2 and put it in a bowl or jar.

2. Tear five pieces, about 1½ inches square, from one napkin or blotter of each color. Put them in the blender with water for recycling, but recycle them only half way. Stop the blender when you can still see clumps of paper.

3. Close the hand mold and put it in the water in the vat.

4. Pour the white pulp into the deckle and stir.

5. Pour the blender's contents into the deckle.

6. Stir slightly with two or three movements of your hand and lift the mold from the vat.

7. Couch and dry as described in chapter 5.

Fig. 6-2 *This sheet was made from the foil wrapping in a box of margarine. The specks are pieces of gold foil.*

Project 2: Glitter and Color with Foil

Recycle a foil food wrapper. The sheet will have bits of foil scattered over it, figure 6-2. Experiment with different food wrappers and with more and less time in the blender. Leave out the white pulp and try a sheet made with only the wrapper.

Materials
- White pulp for ¼ of a sheet (3 strips of 1 x 6-inch white paper will make enough pulp)
- Foil food wrapper

1. Make the white pulp as described in chapter 2 and set it aside.

2. Get the food wrapper as clean as you can. Cut it into small pieces and put them in the blender with water for recycling. Let the blender run until most of the wrapper has been beaten into separate fibers.

3. Close the hand mold and put it in the water in the vat.

4. Pour the white pulp and the food wrapper pulp into the deckle at the same time. Stir to spread the fibers evenly.

5. Lift the mold from the vat.

6. Couch and dry as described in chapter 5.

Chapter 7

Just for fun

The nine projects that follow show how ordinary things—things you can find in your house and in your backyard—can be used to make paper that is really unusual. A leaf, pieces of thread, and a plastic meat tray are some of the things you'll be looking for. Keep your eyes open and your mind thinking as you try these projects. Experience is just as important as directions in learning how to do them. If your paper doesn't turn out well the first time you try a project, don't give up. Ask yourself where—and why—it went wrong and try again. The chances are very good that you'll soon be doing it easily. You'll also find ways to do things that work better for you because you have thought of them. Then you'll begin thinking of new projects to do with fibers, water, and a sieve.

Project 1: Making Paper on Cloth

As you saw in chapter 5, cloth can be laid over your hand mold's screen or hardware cloth. Different cloths give different surfaces to your paper. The weave of the cloth leaves its pattern on the paper's surface. Linen cloth gives paper the texture of linen. Raised patterns on a cloth's surface will make a sheet of paper thicker and thinner in different places. If the sheet is not too thick, you can see the pattern of the cloth in it when you hold the sheet up to the light. Cloths used for couching may also leave a pattern on the paper's surface. Your window screen puts its pattern on the surface of paper made on it.

For this project, choose three pieces of cloth, each having a different weave. Pick one that has a raised pattern of some kind. Carry out the project with each of the three pieces of cloth. Some cloth lets water through faster than others. Don't worry if water drains through the cloth very slowly.

Materials
- 3 pieces of cloth, each 8 inches square
- Pulp for 3 sheets

1. Make pulp by recycling.

2. Open the hand mold and lay a piece of cloth over the screen or hardware cloth. Close the mold. As seen in figure 7-1, the cloth will hang over the sides of the mold.

3. Form a sheet of paper. *Note:* When the mold is set in water, the cloth may not let water rise into the deckle quickly. Dip water into the deckle.

Fig. 7-1 *A sheet can be formed on a piece of cloth put over the screen. The weave of the cloth should be loose enough so that water flows through it easily.*

4. Lay two couch sheets, one on top of the other, on a clean surface. Open the hand mold. Lift the cloth and new sheet by the cloth's upper corners.

5. Holding the cloth straight up, drop its bottom edge near the couch sheet's upper edge (see figure 5-16, page 55). Lower the new sheet onto the couch sheet by bringing your hands toward you and lowering them at the same time. This puts the new sheet and cloth on the couch sheet. The cloth will be on top of the new sheet.

Fig. 7-2 *Before the newly formed sheet is re-moved from the cloth, it is pressed with a rolling pin.*

6.   Use a sponge to press down on the cloth over the entire new sheet. Wring out the sponge. Repeat until the sponge draws no more water.

7.   Place a couch sheet over the cloth. With a rolling pin, roll over the couch sheet four or five times, figure 7-2.

8.   Lift the couch sheet and cloth from the new sheet.

9.   Peel the new sheet from the top of the bottom two couch sheets.

10.   Put the new sheet between two fresh couch sheets and dry it under one or two books. The less

pressure used in drying, the more texture will remain on the surface of the sheet.

11.   When the sheet is dry, see how much the surface has been textured. If a cloth with a raised pattern was used, hold the sheet up to the light and see whether the pattern of the cloth shows in the sheet.

Project 2: Colored Threads 'n Stuff

Make a colorful, pretty sheet by throwing bits of thread into the deckle with the pulp. Some of the thread will end up on the surface of the sheet. The finished sheet should look something like the sheet in figure 7-3.

For different looks, try more or fewer pieces of thread, different lengths, and colored pulp. Try a piece of string with or without threads. Other things to try include broken-up fall leaves, some of your

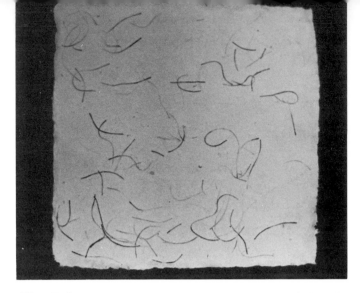

Fig. 7-3 *Threads of different colors can be added to the pulp in the deckle.*

dog's or cat's hair, and sparkly glitter, which you can buy in hobby and art supply stores. Some things look wonderful on sheet surfaces; others look terrible.

Materials
- White pulp for 1 sheet
- 30 to 40 pieces of different-colored threads, ½ to 1 inch long

1. Make the pulp by recycling.

2. Close the hand mold and put it in the water in the vat.

3. Pour the white pulp into the deckle and stir to spread the pulp evenly.

4. Put the pieces of colored thread into the deckle with the pulp and stir again.

5. Lift the deckle from the vat, forming a sheet. Couch and dry as usual.

Project 3: Surface Transplant

Cut a character out of your favorite comic strip and transplant it to the surface of your next sheet of paper. Pictures on gift wrapping paper and greeting cards also make fine transplants. Since it is also made of cellulose fibers, anything cut from paper will bond to a new sheet if put down wet with the fibers, figure 7-4.

Materials
- Pulp for 1 sheet
- Paper cut out that is no larger than ¼ the size of the sheet to which it will be transplanted

Fig. 7-4 *A cut out has been put on the surface of this sheet.*

hand while you stir the pulp in the deckle with your other hand, figure 7-5.

6. Lift the mold from the vat with both hands, but be careful of the cut out.

Fig. 7-5 *Hold the mold and the cut out with one hand, while stirring the pulp with the other.*

1. Make the pulp by recycling.

2. Soak the cut out thoroughly in water.

3. Put the mold in the vat and pour the pulp into the deckle.

4. Decide where you want the cut out to be on the sheet. Hold the cut out by its top between the thumb and forefinger of one hand.

5. Carefully holding the cut out, steady the mold with the same

7. As soon as the water has started to drain, plant the cut out on the screen where you want it to be in the finished sheet. The draining

water and fiber should hold the cut out at the place you put it.

Note: At first, you may find it hard to plant the cut out on the screen with one hand while holding the mold out of the water with the other. If so, try putting two slats across the vat. Rest the mold on the slats while you place the cut out. Slow-draining pulp makes the placement of the cut out easier. Placement is also easier in a thick sheet than in a thin sheet.

8. When the sheet has been formed, lift the mold from the vat. During couching, the cut out may attach itself to the couch sheet and be lifted off the mat of wet fibers. If so, put the couch sheet back down on the mat. With your hand, a thin-bladed screwdriver, or a putty knife, work the cut out off the couch sheet and back onto the mat. Couch and dry as usual.

Project 4: Inside the Paper

Japanese hand papermakers have invented a wonderful kind of paper. A very thin sheet is formed and couched off the screen. On its wet surface are placed leaves, ferns, and even butterflies. Then another thin sheet is formed and couched on top of the first. The natural bond between the fibers holds the two sheets together. This technique can be called double couching. Because the sheets are thin, whatever is put between them shows through.

Fine screens are needed to make thin sheets. If you do not have a fine screen, form the sheets on a piece of cloth. At first, it may be hard for you to make the sheets thin enough, but keep on trying. Use three-fourths as much pulp as you would for a regular sheet. Later, try using even less.

Materials
- Pulp for 2 thin sheets
- Piece of thread 1 foot long
- Flat leaf or flower petal

Fig. 7-6 *A piece of string and a leaf are placed on the surface of a thin sheet that has been couched from the screen. The sheet remains on its couch sheets.*

1.   Make the pulp by recycling.

2.   Soak the string and leaf thoroughly in water.

3.   Make a thin sheet and couch it off the screen onto a couch sheet, removing as little water as possible. If you are forming the sheet on cloth, just lift the cloth and new sheet off the screen and lay them on a clean surface with the new sheet up. Form the second sheet on another cloth.

4.   Place the wet string and leaf on the surface of the newly couched sheet, figure 7-6. Place the string in any design you wish. Gently flatten all of the leaf and string against the sheet's surface.

Fig. 7-7 *The sheet with the string and leaf is used, along with its couch sheets, to couch a second thin sheet from the screen. Line up the edges as closely as possible.*

5. Form a second thin sheet on the screen.

6. Pick up the sheet on which the string and leaf have been placed and use it to couch the second sheet from the screen. When lowering the first sheet on top of the second, line up the edges of the two sheets as exactly as you can, figure 7-7. The sheet with the string

and leaf must be lowered gently and carefully.

7. When the first sheet has been lowered on top of the second, place dry couch sheets on top and apply light pressure with your hands.

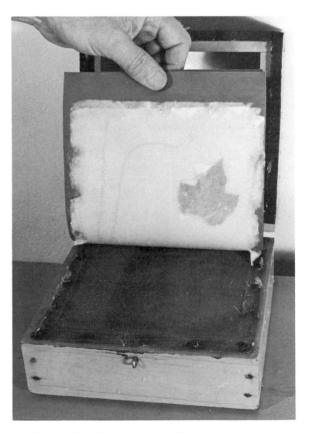

Fig. 7-8 *After more couching, the second sheet rises from the screen with the first.*

9.   Remove more water with dry couch sheets. Press and dry as usual. The final product should look like the sheet shown in figure 7-9.

Project 5: Words in Paper

Instead of a leaf or piece of string, put a word or drawing between the sheets.

Materials
- Pulp for two thin sheets
- 1 piece of clear plastic not larger than 1¼ inches square
- Magic marker or felt tip pen with waterproof ink

1.   Make the pulp by recycling.

2.   Write a word or make a drawing on the clear plastic.

3.   Follow the steps in project 3, placing the plastic between the sheets instead of the leaf and string. When completed, the sheet will

Fig. 7-9 *After further couching and drying, the sheet looks like this.*

8.   Lift the couch sheets carefully. The bottom sheet should have bonded to the first and should rise from the screen, figure 7-8.

Fig. 7-10 *Write or draw something on a piece of clear plastic and put it between paper sheets.*

look like the one shown in figure 7-10.

Project 6: Double Couching with Colored Pulp

By double couching, put a design in colored pulp on a white sheet. To do this, you make a "backwards" cut out called a stencil. It's backwards because you cut out what you want to put on the sheet and throw away the cut out. The piece you have cut *from* is placed in the deckle. When the colored pulp is poured into the deckle, it is forced to flow through the place that has been cut out. Because you want to force the colored pulp through the hole in the stencil, the outside edges of the stencil should touch the sides of the deckle. Make sure you have a tight fit before you start to make paper.

The stencil can be made of wood or any other thin, flat material that will not come apart in water. The plastic foam trays that meat comes in make good stencils. The Christmas tree shape shown in figure 7-11 was made using a cookie cutter as a guide for cutting the stencil. What shapes would you like to put into paper?

Materials
- White pulp for 1 sheet
- Smaller amount of colored pulp (¼ to ⅛ as much as for a sheet, depending on how large the cut-out part of the stencil is)
- Stencil made from waterproof material

Fig. 7-11 *After being formed by a stencil on the screen, fibers in the shape of a Christmas tree are put on a sheet.*

3. Form a sheet with the white pulp and couch it off the screen as usual.

4. Close the hand mold. Put the stencil inside the deckle down on

Fig. 7-12 *The shape of a Christmas tree was cut from the bottom of a plastic meat tray. The tray was cut to fit snugly inside the hand mold and pushed down on top of the screen.*

1. Make the pulp by recycling. If you can't find colored paper to recycle, try project 2 or 3 in chapter 8. But using colored paper will be easier and take less time. Put the white and colored pulp in separate bowls or jars. If you have used a fabric dye to color the pulp, be sure to put the pulp in a glass container.

2. Cut a stencil to fit the deckle, figure 7-12. Remember that the part you cut out and throw away will be the shape in the finished paper. Keep the stencil handy for later use.

top of the screen. The entire surface of the screen should be covered except for the part that has been cut out of the stencil.

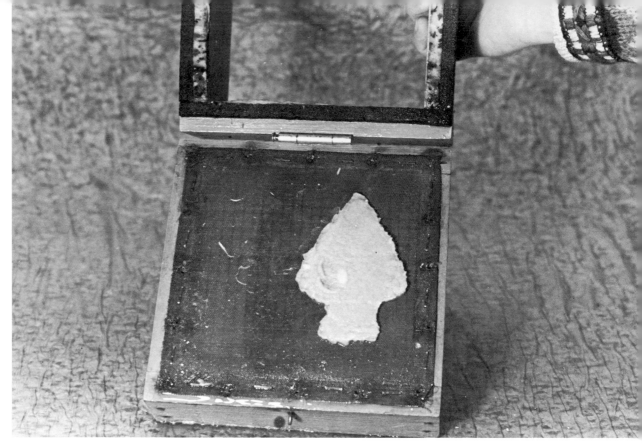

Fig. 7-13 *When the tray is lifted away after making paper, this is what is left. Fibers have been put down on the screen in the image of the cut out.*

5.   Put the mold in the vat. Use one hand to hold the stencil firmly against the screen, especially around the cut-out part. With the other hand, pour the colored pulp into the water in the deckle.

6.   Stir the water in the deckle until the colored pulp is spread evenly. Still holding the stencil firmly against the screen, lift the mold from the vat. The water will run through the screen only where the part is cut out from the stencil, and the fibers will go where the water goes.

7.   Open the mold and carefully remove the stencil. On the screen should be a layer of fibers in the shape that was cut from the stencil, figure 7-13.

8. Use the white sheet you have formed as the couch sheet for couching off the layer of colored fibers. This will put the colored shape on the surface of the white sheet.

9. Remove more water with additional couch sheets. Press and dry as usual.

Project 7: Watermarks

Sometimes, when a sheet of paper is held up to the light, an image can be seen. This is a watermark. Watermarks result from the fiber layer being thinner at some places than at others, letting more light come through the sheet. If the watermark is thicker than the rest of the sheet, it looks darker; if it is thinner, it looks lighter.

Materials
- Pulp for 1 sheet
- 1 plastic twist tie
- Needle and thread
- 1 piece of window screen or cloth cut to fit your mold

1. Roll or twist a flat plastic tie until it is round and bend it into a circle.

2. With needle and thread, sew the circle to the cloth or screen, figure 7-14. Make sure the tie fits

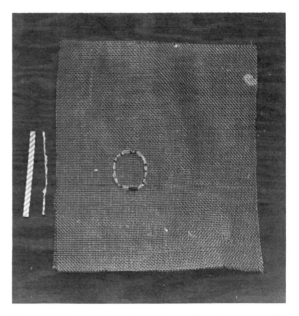

Fig. 7-14 *From left to right: a flat plastic tie, the tie rolled up, and a screen with the tie sewed on its surface.*

tightly against the surfaces so that fibers cannot flow beneath it.

3. Put the screen or cloth on top of the screen on your hand mold and make a sheet of paper.

4. Couch and dry the sheet as usual, but be especially careful when you lift the wet sheet from the screen. If you have formed the sheet on cloth, see page 64 for the couching method to use.

5. When the sheet has dried, hold it up to the light and look at your watermark, figure 7-15. If it is hard to see, make a new sheet that is thinner. If there is a hole where the watermark should be, make a new sheet that is a little thicker.

Project 8: Monogram Your Paper

Use a thin, flexible wire to make a watermark in the shape of your

Fig. 7-15 *The watermark made by a plastic tie sewn to the screen as shown in figure 7-14. To make the watermark show up, the sheet was placed on a piece of glass over a box with a light in it.*

initial. Draw the first letter of your name on a board. At the places where the letter changes its shape, pound small nails into the board. Then bend the wire with a pair of needle-nosed pliers, using the nails as a guide. For ready-made initials, buy pressure-sensitive vinyl plastic letters from an office supply store. You can put the plastic letters directly on the screen of your mold or on a piece of cloth.

Project 9: "Embroidered" Paper

Forming a sheet on embroidered cloth will also make a watermark. Choose a piece of cloth that has an open weave. If you sew it by hand, use embroidery hoops to stretch the cloth, and draw the pattern you want on the cloth first. Put your stitches very close together so that they lie flat and straight against the cloth. Some sewing machines can also make embroidery stitches.

Chapter 8

Dyeing and sizing

Many things can be used to dye and size paper. The paper industry uses dyes and sizes made just for paper, which are not easily available. Hand papermakers have tried many things. From among them, I have chosen several that seem right for projects in this chapter.

Dyeing

Paper can be tinted or dyed. Tints give paper a very light, soft color. Dyes give paper a deeper color.

Be careful when you handle tints and dyes. Anything touched by water that has a tint or dye in it can be stained. Avoid splashing. Wear old clothes or something over good clothes when dyeing or tinting. Soap and water clean up some dyes, but fabric dyes stain most things permanently. Be extra careful with fabric dyes and use only glass containers.

Tints and dyes also stain couch sheets. Set certain couch sheets aside for use only in making colored paper. If you use stained couch sheets to make white paper, the white paper will be stained.

Do not lay tinted or dyed sheets directly on your work surface. If you do, staining can occur. Keep a couch sheet between dyed sheets and work surfaces.

Most of the time you will find it easier and safer to make colored sheets by using fibers recycled from colored papers. But there might be a time when you want a certain color or a deeper, brighter color that you can get only by tinting or dyeing.

For tinting, try using food coloring. It can be found in food stores next to the sugar, flour, and baking mixes.

For dyeing, this chapter suggests two types of dyes—pigment and fabric. Pigment can be bought at art supply stores. Ask for "acrylic artists colors." Acrylic colors are easy to use. Unlike tints and some dyes, they can be cleaned up with soap and water. When dissolved in water, fabric dyes give their color permanently to materials. They can deeply stain such things as wooden spoons, plastic spoons, and containers. When using fabric dyes, be very careful. They are sold at supermarkets, variety stores, and fabric shops.

Following are projects for tinting with food coloring, dyeing with pigment, and dyeing with fabric dye.

Project 1: Tinting with Food Coloring

Materials
- White paper for recycling—enough to make 1 new sheet

- 1 cup water
- ½ teaspoon food coloring

1. Cut the white paper to be recycled into small pieces. Put the pieces into the blender.

2. To the paper in the blender, add 1 cup water and ½ teaspoon food coloring.

3. Turn the blender on and let it run until the paper pieces are recycled into fibers.

4. Make a sheet of paper with the tinted fibers as usual.

Project 2: Dyeing with Acrylic Artists Colors

Materials
- White paper for recycling—enough to make 1 sheet

- 1 cup water
- ¼ teaspoon acrylic artists color

1. Cut the white paper to be recycled into small pieces. Put the pieces into the blender.

2. To the paper in the blender, add 1 cup of water and ¼ teaspoon of acrylic artists color.

3. Turn the blender on and let it run until the paper pieces are recycled into fibers. Foam may appear in the blender, but it is nothing to worry about.

4. Make a sheet of paper with the dyed fibers as usual.

Project 3: Dyeing with Fabric Dye

Materials
- White paper for recycling—enough to make 1 new sheet
- 1 cup hot water
- ¼ teaspoon fabric dye
- Glass jar or bowl

1. Pour 1 cup hot water into a glass jar or bowl.

2. Add ¼ teaspoon fabric dye to the water in the jar. Stir until the dye grains are completely dissolved, about 2 to 3 minutes. Use a stirrer you can throw away or a metal spoon. Dye stains wooden and plastic spoons.

3. Cut the paper to be recycled into small pieces. Add the pieces to the water and dye in the jar.

4. Let the paper stand in the dye for about 15 minutes. Stir often so that the dye spreads evenly among the paper pieces.

5. Pour the dye and paper into the blender. Be careful not to splash. Be sure to put the lid on the blender before you turn it on.

6.   Turn the blender on and let it run until the paper pieces are completely recycled into fibers.

7.   Make a sheet of paper with dyed fibers as in chapter 5. Note that in step 2 under "Couching," you may not want to put your hands directly on the couch sheets. Put a piece of plastic or a flat board between your hands and the couch sheet. This will keep your hands from getting stained.

Sizing

Without sizing, paper acts somewhat like a blotter. As ink or watercolor paints are put on paper's surface, they are blotted into the paper. This makes the edges of the written lines blur instead of staying straight and sharp and is called "feathering."

Sizing puts a coating around fibers or on a sheet's surface. The coating makes the paper less like a blotter. Heavy sizing keeps paper from blotting hardly at all.

The thinner, or more liquid, paint or ink is, the more likely feathering will happen. Ballpoint ink does not usually feather even on unsized papers.

You can size papers in a number of ways, as shown in the following projects. When sizing paper, protect the work surface with a dry couch sheet. It makes cleanup easier.

Often paper you recycle will be sized. The new sheet made from the recycled fibers will keep some of the sizing.

Project 4: Sizing with Aerosol Spray

This project makes a heavily sized sheet. Either of two sprays can be used: a fabric protector such as Scotchgard, or a silicone spray for waterproofing shoes.

Fig. 8-1 *For spraying, rest sheet on four nails pounded into an old board. Stand the board upright by leaning it against something.*

Materials
- 1 can of fabric protector or silicone aerosol spray
- 1 handmade sheet of paper at least 5 days old

1. Find a place where you can spray. It can be outdoors or in a big room that is well ventilated.

2. Put a handmade sheet at least 5 days old where it can be sprayed. Hang it on a line with a clip clothespin, or lean it against a board that will not be hurt by the spray, figure 8-1.

3. Follow all directions on the aerosol spray can. Spray the sheet

until you see that its entire surface has been covered.

4.   Let the paper dry for 10 minutes. Then turn the paper around and spray the other side.

5.   Let the sheet dry. This should give you a sheet on which liquid ink will not feather. If feathering still occurs, give the sheet a second coating. Experience will be your best guide on how much spray to put on a sheet.

Project 5: Sizing with Gelatin

Gelatin provides light sizing. You can use one batch of sizing for many sheets. Unflavored gelatin, used in food, can be found with the gelatin desserts and pudding mixes in the supermarket.

Materials
- Handmade paper that is at least 5 days old
- 1½ cups water
- 1 envelope unflavored gelatin
- 1 saucepan
- 1 cake pan or pie tin just large enough so that the sheet of paper can lie flat in it
- 4 pieces of cloth, each at least as big as the handmade paper

1.   Heat 1½ cups water to boiling in a saucepan. Take it off the stove.

2.   Add 1 tablespoon unflavored gelatin to the boiling water and stir until it is completely dissolved.

3.   Pour the gelatin into the cake pan or pie tin. Let it cool until you can put your finger into it comfortably. If it cools too much, it will become thick like Jello. If this happens, put it back in the saucepan and heat it until it thins out again.

4.   Put a sheet of paper in the gel-

atin and hold it under the surface for about 2 minutes. The gelatin must be deep enough to cover the paper.

5. Remove the sheet and place it on a piece of cloth to dry. The bonds between the fibers have been weakened by the moisture, so handle the sheet carefully.

6. After an hour, move the sheet to a dry cloth.

7. When the sheet is almost dry, put it between two pieces of cloth. Put the cloths between two couch sheets. Finish drying under books or other weight.

8. Repeat steps 4 through 7 for each sheet you want to size. Keep the gelatin from stiffening by keeping it warm.

Project 6: Sizing with Liquid Starch

Clothes starch, found with detergents and bleaches in supermarkets, will size paper lightly. Liquid clothes starch works well, and many sheets can be sized with one batch of starch. When you are finished, pour the starch back into the bottle for re-use. Spray and powder starches are discussed at the end of this project.

Materials
- Handmade paper at least 5 days old
- 1 cake or pie tin just large enough so that the sheet of paper can lie flat in it
- 1½ cups liquid clothes starch
- 4 pieces of cloth, each at least as large as your handmade sheet
- 2 couch sheets

1. Pour 1½ cups liquid starch into a cake or pie tin.

2. Slip a sheet of handmade paper beneath the surface of the starch.

3.   Hold the sheet under the surface for 2 to 3 minutes.

4.   Take the paper out of the starch. The fiber bonds will be weakened from the moisture, so handle the paper carefully.

5.   For drying the paper, follow steps 5 through 7 of project 5. Because starch is sticky, your sized sheet might stick to the cloths that you use for drying. Be careful when you separate the sheet and the cloth.

Use spray starch if you wish. It is a light sizing. Follow the steps given for aerosol sprays in project 4.

Powdered starches can also be used. Simply put ½ to 1 teaspoonful into the blender, along with 1 cup of water, when you recycle paper. Powdered starches may not provide a sizing as heavy as others.

Any sheet you size by any methods given in these projects can be given another "coating." Just run the same sheet through the process again.

Fig. 9-1 *In a painting made around 1780, Chinese papermakers dry their paper by brushing the wet sheets onto mud or stucco slabs heated by a fire. To the left are two papermakers using a large hand mold. Behind them is a man pressing water out of the sheets before they are put on the heated slabs.*

Chapter 9

Drying on a board and in a press

Board Drying

The oldest traditions in making paper by hand are in China, Korea, and Japan, in that order. Some of these ways have not changed in almost two thousand years. Lacking gas or electricity for heat, Oriental papermakers found other ways to heat flat surfaces for drying their paper, figure 9-1. Sometimes they did not even use heat. They put their new, wet sheets on boards to dry. Some of the finest paper in the world has been made in these age-old ways. You can keep the tradition alive in your time.

Board drying prevents wavy edges and puckering that might otherwise occur as paper dries. It also transfers the texture of the board to the paper. The first time you try drying on a board, choose one that is smooth. It can be painted, varnished, or unfinished. The next time choose one that has a raised pattern you can feel with your hand. Boards that are not sanded smooth or that are worn from being outdoors are apt to have raised patterns. Look for knots that have grain lines swirling around them. Figure 9-2 shows paper drying on a rough board.

Project 1: Board Drying

1. Clean the board to remove all dust and dirt.

Fig. 9-2 *Board drying. While very wet, this sheet was couched from a couch sheet onto this rough, unsanded board. The pattern of ridges and lines on the board's surface will be transferred to the surface of the paper. The sheet will be left on the board until completely dry.*

2.   Dampen the board's surface.

3.   Form a sheet of paper on a piece of cloth or on a loose screen.

4.   Lift the cloth or screen from the mold by the upper corners. Drop the bottom edge of the cloth or screen onto the board (see figure 5-16, page 55). By lowering your hands and pulling them towards you, drop the sheet gently onto the board's surface.

5.   Press the back of the cloth or screen lightly with your hand or a wet sponge so that the new sheet is pushed against the board.

6.   Raise one corner of the cloth carefully. Lift it just high enough to see whether or not the sheet stays on the board. If it does, lift the rest of the cloth or screen away from the sheet. If it does not stay on the board, keep trying at different places around the edge until you find a place where the new sheet does not rise.

7.   Let the paper dry naturally. Don't put anything on top of it, and don't apply heat. Drying might take two days or longer.

Paper Presses

As you have found by stacking weights on top of newly formed sheets, pressure makes paper dry smoothly. For this reason, many papermakers use pressure for drying.

A press can apply more pressure than weights can. It is especially good for paper that has been made by double couching and for paper that has had something transplanted to its surface. Paper dried under a lot of pressure has edges that are flat and smooth. Its surface is also smoother than paper dried under little pressure.

Fig. 9-3 *A press used by hand paper-makers of the past. It is about twelve feet high.*

When paper was made by hand, paper mills had huge presses built especially for them, figure 9-3. Today, hand papermakers can sometimes find old presses used by other trades such as printing and bookbinding. But the easiest and cheapest way to get a press is to build one.

With a small jack, like those used for changing tires on cars, you can build a press that costs less

nut

washer

Fig. 9-4 *Home-built press. The platforms are held in place on rods
by washers and nuts. The hydraulic jack is pumped up
against the top platform. A
piece of wood has been placed
on the small top of the jack.
The jack's base presses down
on flat boards. Between the
boards are wet sheets between
couch sheets. The wet sheets
are held absolutely flat while
drying.*

than twenty dollars. It is shown in figure 9-4. You will probably need the help of someone who is skilled with tools.

Project 2: Building a Paper Press

The press built in this project is big enough for paper sheets 8 inches square. For larger sheets, make larger platforms that are at least 4 inches bigger than the paper you want to press.

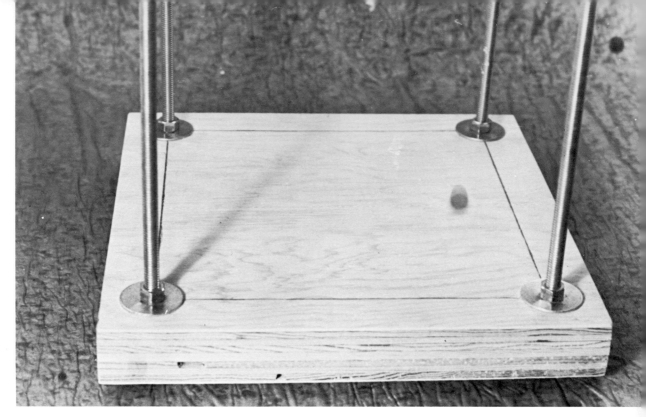

Fig. 9-5 *Four lines are drawn 1½ inches in from each edge. Where they cross near the corners is the place to drill a hole for the threaded rods.*

Materials

- Small hydraulic jack
- 4 pieces of ¾-inch plywood, 1 foot square
- 2 threaded rods, ⅜ inch in diameter and 36 inches long
- 16 nuts, ⅜ inch
- 16 washers, ⅜-inch hole, 1½ inches wide overall
- Steel plate at least 3 inches square (You can use the base section of a large metal hinge or a 4-inch length of 2 x 4 lumber in place of the plate.)

1. Glue two of the pieces of plywood together, making a platform 1½ inches thick. Clamp the pieces together or put weights on them until the glue has dried.

2. Do the same with the other two pieces of plywood. The platforms will last longer if you put a waterproof paint or varnish on them.

3. Draw a line across each platform 1½ inches in from each edge. Where the lines cross at each

corner, drill a ⅜-inch hole, figure 9-5.

4.   Cut the two threaded rods in half, making 4 threaded rods, each 18 inches long. If you haven't cut threaded rods, get help from someone who has.

5.   Put the platforms on the rods with nuts and washers in the following order: (a) nut; (b) washer; (c) platform; (d) washer; and (e) nut. This will place a platform on each rod end between two washers held tightly together by two nuts, figure 9-6. If it is hard to thread the rods through the holes, drill the holes again with a $^{13}/_{32}$ or $^{7}/_{16}$-inch drill bit.

Fig. 9-6 *Put a nut and washer above and below each of the four rods.*

Fig. 9-7 *Put a steel plate on the bottom of the upper platform.*

6.   The top of the jack's piston is small, and the pressure it puts against the top platform of the press must be spread over a greater area. If possible, get a piece of steel plate 3 inches square or larger. Fasten it with screws to the center of the top platform's bottom surface, figure 9-7. If you don't have a steel plate, use the base section of a large metal hinge. If you don't have a hinge, place a 4-inch length of 2 x 4 lumber on top of the jack.

Project 3: Using the Paper Press

1.   When a sheet has been couched from the screen, remove enough water so that it can be lifted from the couch sheet. Place the wet

sheet between dry couch sheets and put them between two flat boards.

2.   Place the boards on the bottom platform of the press and the jack on top of the boards.

3.   Pump the jack's piston up against the bottom of the top platform. If the piston does not reach the top platform, put more pieces of board under the jack, figure 9-4, page 91. Apply pressure for 3 to 5 minutes. To keep water from run-

ning back into the sheet when the pressure is released, brush the edges of the couch sheets with a damp sponge.

4.   Release the jack. Put the paper between dry couch sheets and put it back into the press. Apply pressure for at least 2 to 3 hours or overnight.

5.   Change the couch sheets again. Apply pressure for 4 to 5 hours or until paper is dry.

Chapter 10

Make it like a craftsman

Handmade paper can be made either by the pour or the dip method. In the pour method, which you have been using, the fibers and water are poured into a deckle above the screen. In the dip method the fibers and water are put into a vat, and the screen is dipped into the mixture. Since the water and fibers are held in a vat, the deckle for the dip method is shallow, hardly more than a rim around the edge of the screen.

The dip method is the only method used by European and American papermakers of the past. Outside of some places in Tibet and the South Seas, those who made paper for a living used the dip method.

By 1800 the handmade paper industry had reached its peak in Europe. Building a dip hand mold, figure 10-1, was almost as much of

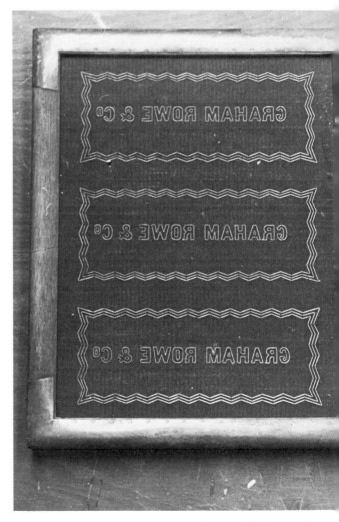

Fig. 10-1 *A mold made for a mill that made paper by hand in England. On it is the watermark of the customer for which this mold was used.*

an art as making paper. Highly skilled carpenters used costly woods like mahogany and teak, which resist water damage, and rustproof fittings of copper, brass, and bronze. Some molds were very small. Some were large enough so that more than one sheet could be made at each dipping. Still others were so large that two workers were needed to do the dipping. Finishing processes, such as sizing, were done with such care that it was usually three months between the time a wet sheet was formed and the time it was ready for a customer.

To find out about the building of fine dip molds, read *Papermaking by Hand in 1967* by J. Barcham Green. Mr. Green is a craftsman with Hayle Mill in Maidstone, Kent, England. Hayle Mill is one of the few remaining handmade paper mills in Europe, and Mr. Green's family has been making paper since the late 1600s. If you would like to see dip hand molds of long ago, visit the Dard Hunter Paper Museum in Appleton, Wisconsin.

Today, most dip hand molds cost more than one hundred dollars. See the appendix, page 107, for places to buy one.

With modern materials, you can make a very simple dip mold. It will not be as fancy, strong, or good as the traditional dip molds. But you won't make paper with it ten hours a day, six days a week, as the craftsmen of the past did with theirs.

Project 1: Building a Dip Hand Mold

Materials

- Wood pieces of the following types and sizes:
    ¾ x 1½-inch blind stock, 36 inches long
    ½ x ¾-inch parting stop, 40 inches long
    ¼ x 1¾-inch lattice strip, 14 inches long

- 6 corner irons, 1½ x ⅜ inch
- Hardware cloth, 6¾ x 8 inches
- Window screen, 6¾ x 8 inches (If you want to use papermaking wire instead, see the appendix, page 107, for ordering information.)
- Paint

1. Cut the blind stock into 2 pieces 8 ⁷⁄₁₆ inches long and 2 pieces 5 ¾ inches long. Put the short pieces between the ends of the longer pieces to form a frame and nail or glue them together. This will be the frame for the screen, figure 10-2.

2. Cut the parting stop into 2 pieces 9 ⁹⁄₁₆ inches long and 2 pieces 7 ¼ inches long. Put the short pieces between the ends of the longer pieces and nail or glue them together. This will be the frame for the deckle, figure 10-2.

Fig. 10-2 *From left to right: the screen frame, the deckle frame, and the top of the deckle frame. The two frames on the left are assembled. Note that the short pieces of wood go between the ends of the longer pieces. The two frames on the left have corner irons for bracing. The frame to the right is unassembled. It will be fitted, piece by piece, on top of the deckle frame.*

3. Put the larger frame (deckle) around the smaller frame (screen), figure 10-3. The fit should be close, but one frame should not bind on the other. If it does, sand the inside of the deckle frame and outside of the screen frame until they fit. If the fit is still too tight, check your measurements and rebuild the deckle or screen frame. Paint the frames after you get a good fit.

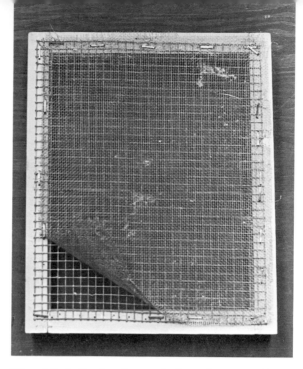

Fig. 10-4 *Put hardware cloth on the screen frame first. Put window screen on top of the hardware cloth.*

4. Put a corner iron on two diagonally opposite corners of the deckle frame and on all four corners of the screen frame, figure 10-3.

5. Turn the screen frame over. Staple the hardware cloth to the frame or tack it with no. 6 carpet tacks. Put the window screen on top of the hardware cloth and staple it to the frame, figure 10-4, or tack it with no. 4 copper screen tacks. This completes the screen frame of the dip mold.

Fig. 10-3 *The deckle frame must fit closely around the screen frame, but it should not bind. The deckle frame should part from the screen quite easily.*

Fig. 10-5 *A piece of the lattice strip is lined up on top of the deckle frame.*

Fig. 10-6 *Two short pieces of lattice strip are added to the top of the deckle frame. When in the right place, the strips are tacked down with two nails.*

Fig. 10-7 *The last piece of lattice strip is fitted into place. Changes are made as needed before the final nailing.*

6. Cut the lattice strip into 2 pieces 9 $^9\!/_{16}$ inches long and 2 pieces 5 $^9\!/_{16}$ inches long. Paint all 4 pieces. Put one 9 $^9\!/_{16}$-inch strip on top of one 9 $^9\!/_{16}$-inch side of the deckle frame. Line up the outside edges carefully. The lattice strip must cover the inside edges of the deckle frame. (During papermaking, the lattice part of the deckle frame rests on the window screen. It determines the size of the paper sheet.) Fasten the strip lightly with two nails to hold it in place, figure 10-5.

7. Put the shorter lattice strips on the shorter sides of the deckle frame and line up the outside edges. Butt them against the inside edges of the long piece, figure 10-6, and fasten them lightly in place with two nails each.

8. Put the remaining long lattice strip in place on top of the deckle frame, figure 10-7. Make sure that

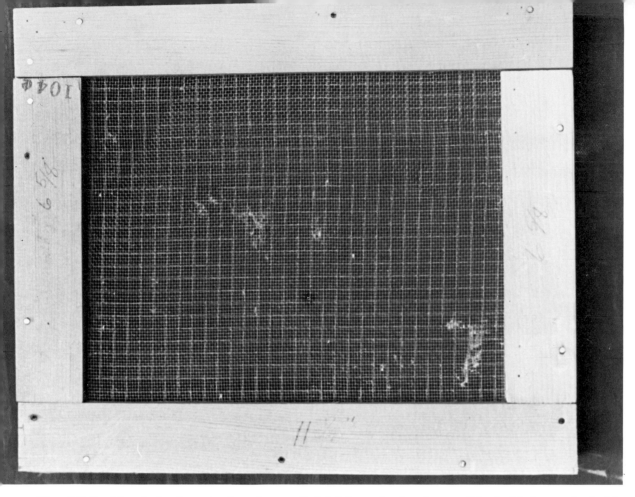

Fig. 10-8 *After the lattice strips have been nailed tightly or glued to the top of the deckle frame, the deckle is put around the screen.*

the lattice frame fits well on top of the deckle frame. If not, remove the nails and center the lattice frame on the deckle frame. When the two frames match exactly, nail or glue them together. This completes the deckle of the dip mold.

9. Fit the deckle over the screen.

The mold is now ready for making paper, figure 10-8.

Project 2: Dipping a Sheet

In the dip method, pulp and water are put into a vat. The hand mold is dipped into the vat and removed. As soon as the sheet is couched off the screen, the mold can be dipped again to make another sheet. As the pulp-water mixture in the vat grows thinner, more pulp is added.

Materials

- Vat: a plastic dishpan that has inside measurements of 13 inches long, 11¼ inches wide, and 5½ inches deep
- 7½ quarts water
- 2 full newspaper sheets, each measuring 29 x 23¼ inches, or an equal amount of other paper. (If you have a postage scale, or a good kitchen scale, get about 1¾ ounces of dry paper of any kind to equal the newspaper sheets.)
- ½ full sheet of newspaper (This equals about ¼ ounce of dry paper of any kind.)
- Kitchen strainer
- Dip hand mold
- Couch sheets or felts measuring 8 x 9 inches

1.   Recycle two full newspaper sheets, or other kinds of paper, into

Fig. 10-9 *The dip method starts with the mold held straight up and down over the vat containing the pulp.*

fibers. With a kitchen strainer, drain most of the water from the recycled fibers.

2.   Place the fibers in a plastic dishpan, which will serve as your vat. Add 7½ quarts of water to the vat.

3.   Put the deckle around the screen of your dip mold. Stir the pulp and water in the vat with your hands or a paddle. This will cause the fibers to spread around evenly in the water, which in turn will help you make a sheet that is the same thickness all over. Stir briskly.

4.   Hold the dip mold straight up

and down over the vat, figure 10-9. Bring it down into the vat and under the surface of the water and fibers. When it is almost, or totally, beneath the surface, turn the mold to a flat position, bringing its bottom towards you, figure 10-10.

Fig. 10-10 *The mold is slid down into the pulp and then turned to a flat (horizontal) position under the surface of the pulp.*

5. Keeping the mold flat, lift it out of the vat, figure 10-11. The deckle will trap the pulp on top of the screen. As the water drains, shake the mold gently front to back and

sideways. This helps spread the fibers evenly around on the screen and helps them bond better to one another.

6. After the water has stopped draining, remove the deckle from the screen.

7. Lay a couch sheet on a flat surface. If you use a couch felt instead, make sure that it is damp.

8. Hold the screen with the formed sheet straight up and down and place one long edge of the

Fig. 10-11 *The mold is raised straight up out of the pulp. It is kept level. The lattice frame, which is part of the deckle, keeps the pulp from running off the sides of the screen.*

screen against one long edge of the couch sheet, figure 10-12.

9.   Holding the edge of the frame firmly against the couch sheet, lower the screen gently. If the

Fig. 10-12 *One side of the screen frame is put down on the edge of the couch sheet.*

screen slips or slides as it is lowered, the newly formed sheet will probably be ruined. Press down on the screen frame so that the new sheet transfers from the screen to the couch sheet, figure 10-13. Do not let the screen slip or slide at

Fig. 10-13 *The screen is put flat down on the couch sheet, pressing the newly formed sheet onto the couch sheet.*

any time it is touching the new sheet.

10.   To complete the couching, raise the mold as shown in figure 10-14. *Note:* If couching is difficult, couch the sheet in the same way you did when using your pour hand mold.

Fig. 10-14 *The side of the screen that was put down first is lifted up first. The newly formed sheet stays on the couch sheet.*

11.   As soon as you have couched the sheet off the screen, put a dry couch sheet on top of it. Then make another sheet and couch it off onto the couch sheet on top of the first sheet. Doing the same thing, make two more sheets. You will then have a stack of four new sheets with couch sheets between them. Put a couch sheet on top of the stack.

12.   After dipping several sheets, you will have fewer fibers in your vat, but about the same amount of water. This means that the next sheets you make will be thinner. After every fourth sheet that you dip, recycle one half of one full sheet of newspaper, or about ¼-ounce dry weight of other kinds of paper, and add the fibers to the vat. Then make four more sheets.

13.   Press and dry the newly formed sheets. Put a flat, clean board that is at least as large as the top couch sheet over them and press on the board with your hands. For more weight, stand on the board. Repeat this step once or twice, each time replacing the wet couch sheets with dry ones. Then dry as usual. If you made a paper press, follow the directions given for using it in chapter 9, page 94. All the sheets can be pressed at once. Replace wet couch sheets with dry ones between pressings.

Appendix

Buying Information

The source for professional materials and equipment associated with the pour hand mold (described in Chapter 4) is the author's paper craft company, Greg Markim, Inc.

Professional materials and equipment available are as follows:

Couch sheets (blotters)
Papermaking screens
Pour hand molds
Direction sheet (poster-size, printed
          waterproof paper)
Video - 57 minutes, shows how to
          make paper with the pour
          hand mold, recycling, more.
Tin Can Papermaking Packet - special
          packet of professional materials
          for making paper as in Chapter 1.
Complete Papermaking Kit - professionally built hand mold and all necessary materials for making paper as shown in this book. Makes a 6x8-inch sheet or an 8½x11-inch sheet.

Answers to questions about hand papermaking.
    Address: Greg Markim, Inc.
                 Box 183
                 Appleton, WI 54912
                 Tel. 414/734-9678

Other Supplies and Suppliers

Listed below are three well-established suppliers. Between them, they handle most anything a hand papermaker can want. Write for information and a catalog. Enclosing a 25-cent stamp, to help defray expense of mailing materials, is always appreciated.

Hand papermaking supplies and equipment include dip hand molds, papermaking screens, couch felts, dyes and pigments, sizing agents, new pulp of a wide range of standard domestic and exotic foreign fibers, beaters, hydraulic presses, etc.

Twinrocker Handmade Paper
Box 413
Brookston, Indiana 47923
Telephone 317/563-3119
          317/563-3210

Carriage House Paper
at Brickbottom
1 Fitchburg Street #C-207
Somerville, MA 02143
Tel. 617/629-2337

Lee S. McDonald Inc.
P.O. Box 264
Charlestown, MA 02129
Tel. 617/242-2505

Commercial Paper Industry Information

Addresses of most any company in, or allied to, the commercial paper industry, including basic manufacturers of felts, screen, etc., can be found in the annual *Lockwood's Directory of the Paper and Allied Trades.*

Index